I0427147

SECRETS TO MAKING MILLIONS WITH AFFILIATE MARKETING

A Millionaire's Blueprint to six figures

By

Genevieve Allan

Copyright © 2024 Genevieve Allan
All Right reserved

Table of Contents

INTRODUCTION

Welcome to the exciting world of making money through affiliate marketing! I'm here to help you learn the tips and tricks that can turn you into a millionaire. We'll talk about things like how to think like a millionaire, how affiliate marketing works, and what you need to do to succeed. Join me as we explore picking the right niche, creating great content, and teaming up with others to reach millionaire status in affiliate marketing.

Chapter 1

Introduction to Affiliate Marketing

In the vast realm of online entrepreneurship, affiliate marketing presents itself as a lucrative opportunity, offering a journey towards financial success from start to finish. This segment acts as your guide, leading you through the complex terrain of affiliate marketing and revealing the undisclosed tactics essential for attaining monetary abundance.

By Definition

Affiliate marketing involves a collaborative strategy built on a mutually advantageous partnership between merchants and affiliates. In this arrangement, merchants supply goods or services, while affiliates strategically promote these offerings across different platforms, earning commissions for every sale or lead they generate. This simple yet impactful concept forms the foundation for the possibility of substantial financial gains.

Who' is an affiliate?

An affiliate refers to an individual or entity collaborating with a merchant or business to advertise and sell their products or services. Commissions earned by these affiliates are contingent on particular actions, such as sales, clicks, or leads, stemming from their promotional efforts. Affiliates commonly use unique links or tracking codes to accurately monitor and credit these activities. The spectrum of affiliates extends from individual bloggers and influencers to large marketing companies, playing a pivotal role in broadening a business's outreach and improving sales through effective promotional strategies.

Who is a Merchant

A vendor or trader is referred to as an individual, company, or organization that displays goods or services for purchase. In the realm of affiliate marketing, vendors establish alliances with affiliates to advertise and distribute their products. Typically, affiliates are furnished with unique tracking links or codes by vendors to monitor the effectiveness of their promotional efforts in generating sales or leads. This cooperative arrangement proves advantageous for both parties: vendors gain heightened exposure and sales, while affiliates receive commissions for steering customers towards the vendor's offerings.

Relatable example

Consider a situation where you're scrolling through a social media platform and come across a lifestyle blogger's post endorsing a particular brand of workout gear. Intrigued, you click on the provided link which directs you to an online store where these products are sold.

Little do you know, the blogger is actually an affiliate for that online store. When you click on their affiliate link and make a purchase, you not only get the fitness equipment you were interested in but also contribute to the blogger's earnings. Every sale made through their unique affiliate link earns the blogger a commission.

In our daily routines, whether it's buying workout gear or suggesting a store to a friend, we inadvertently play a role in the affiliate marketing system.

What many don't realize is that they, too, have the potential to earn significant income by participating in similar activities, thus establishing a passive income stream for themselves.

Why venture into the affiliate marketing journey?

The essence lies in its unparalleled scalability and accessibility. Departing from traditional business models, affiliate marketing offers an avenue to entrepreneurship with minimal upfront expenses, making it accessible to both novices and seasoned marketers aiming for financial prosperity.

As we uncover the complexities of affiliate marketing, you will recognize the importance of strategic alliances. Succeeding in this field hinges on the ability to identify profitable niches, choose reputable affiliate programs, and produce compelling content that resonates with your audience. Progressing from initiation to financial success requires not only a deep understanding of the endorsed products but also expertise in persuasive communication, particularly in copywriting.

In the following sections, we will explore how individuals, through their everyday online or offline activities, may inadvertently engage in and promote affiliate marketing endeavors. Brace yourself for an expedition through the ever-evolving realm of affiliate marketing. Whether you are a beginner aspiring for financial autonomy or a seasoned marketer pursuing higher objectives, this chapter lays the groundwork for advancing from inception to financial success in affiliate marketing.

Let's bandy the process of opting the applicable niche and products for your trip as an affiliate marketer, with the goal of achieving significant success. Choosing the Right Niche for Your Affiliate Marketing Venture opting the right niche is a pivotal original step towards a marketing trip, holding significant sway over your implicit success, particularly on platforms similar as Amazon. A niche refers to a specific member of the request distinguished by participated interests or characteristics. When determining the optimal niche for your chapter marketing trials, consider the following factors

1. Passion and Knowledge

Select a specialized area that resonates with your passions or unique strengths. Genuine enthusiasm for your chosen topic not only amplifies your enjoyment of the work but also empowers you to impart valuable insights to your audience. Evaluate the inherent followership in your selected niche, confirming the demand for products or information associated with it. Understanding the needs and preferences of your target audience is essential for effectively tailoring your marketing strategies.

2. Competition Analysis

Conduct a thorough analysis of the competitive landscape within your industry. While healthy competition can be beneficial, operating in an oversaturated market presents challenges in establishing your distinct identity. Aim for a harmonious equilibrium that allows you to carve out a recognizable presence within the niche.

3. Profitability potential

Assess the potential profitability of your chosen niche by examining the commission rates offered through affiliate programs in that sector. Certain niches may offer greater earning potential, attracting affiliate marketers.

4. Evergreen vs Trending niche

Determine whether your chosen niche is evergreen or subject to fleeting trends. Evergreen niches maintain enduring popularity, whereas trending niches may yield rapid success but risk fading over time. A combination of both provides stability and avenues for growth.

5. Merchant Reputation

Forge partnerships with reputable merchants and affiliate programs in your chosen field. Your credibility as an affiliate marketer is contingent upon the reputation of the products or services you endorse.

6. Diversity of product

Opt for a niche that allows for a diverse array of products, affording flexibility and the opportunity to explore various affiliate offerings that resonate with different segments of your audience.

Selecting the optimal niche for your affiliate marketing venture is a deliberate process that encompasses personal interest, audience relevance, profitability, and strategic planning. By carefully considering these factors, you can position yourself for success in the competitive realm of affiliate marketing.

Selecting the right products as an affiliate

Selecting the right products as an affiliate is a critical aspect of achieving success in the realm of affiliate marketing. It requires strategic decision-making to pinpoint products that resonate with the needs and preferences of your target audience. Key considerations include the product's relevance to your niche, its quality, and the reputation of the merchant offering it. Furthermore, analyzing the demand for the product and understanding your audience's purchasing behavior can assist in selecting products with the highest potential for conversion. Ultimately, a thoughtful and well-informed approach to product selection increases the likelihood of crafting a successful affiliate marketing campaign.

Choosing reputable affiliate programs is essential in constructing a successful affiliate marketing strategy. It entails a comprehensive evaluation of various factors to ensure alignment with trustworthy, ethical, and goal-oriented programs. The following guide offers comprehensive insights into this process:

1. Evaluate Merchant Reputation:

Conduct thorough research into the reputation of merchants or businesses offering affiliate programs. Opt for well-regarded entities with positive reviews, a track record of timely payments, and a commitment to ethical business practices.

2. Assess Commission Structure:

Examine the commission structure of potential affiliate programs, aiming for fairness and competitiveness within the industry. Exercise caution with programs offering overly high commissions, as this could signal sustainability issues or potential challenges.

3.Examine Cookie Duration

Inspect the cookie duration, which indicates the time frame during which you can potentially earn a commission after a user clicks on your affiliate link. A longer cookie duration extends the opportunity for conversions.

4. Ensure product or service quality

Ensure the quality of the product or service
by associating with affiliate programs that offer high-quality offerings. Your promotional efforts directly impact your credibility, so collaborate with merchants who meet or exceed industry standards.

5. Review payment terms and schedule

It is very important to review the payment terms or potential affiliate programs, favoring those with transparent payment procedures that ensure regular and timely payments. Reliable programs clearly outline payment methods and frequency.

6. Consider the level of support and resources

The level of support provided by affiliate programs. Trustworthy programs typically supply promotional materials, tracking tools, and specialized assistance to enhance the effectiveness of your marketing efforts.

7. Examine Merchant -Affiliate track record

Examine the track record of merchants and affiliate programs by gathering feedback from fellow affiliates who have partnered with them. Utilize online forums, reviews, and testimonials to gain valuable insights into the experiences of other affiliate marketers.

8. Scrutinize Terms and conditions

Scrutinize the terms and conditions of affiliate programs, paying close attention to any restrictions, exclusions, or clauses that may impact your ability to earn commissions.

9. Prioritize transparency and communication

Prioritize transparency and communication by selecting affiliate programs that emphasize openness in their transactions. Clear communication and well-defined guidelines foster a positive and collaborative relationship between affiliates and merchants.

10. Verify affiliate program

Verify that the chosen affiliate program complies with relevant regulations and industry standards, including adherence to privacy policies, anti-spam laws, and other legal requirements.

Chapter 2

Introduction to Building a Wealth Mindset

Welcome to the illuminating journey of "Fostering a Wealth Mindset." Within this thorough exploration of financial empowerment, we embark on a transformative path that extends beyond mere wealth accumulation. This expedition goes deeper into the complex psychology underlying wealth creation, emphasizing the profound impact of one's mindset on financial outcomes.

Grasping the Concept of a Wealth Mindset starts with a deep examination of the essential traits characterizing a wealth mindset. Rather than solely fixating on monetary gain, it should be a holistic approach. This approach involves seizing opportunities, cultivating a steadfast belief in abundance, and adeptly maneuvering through obstacles. You will meticulously uncover   the core principles that differentiate a wealth mindset from a scarcity mindset, offering nuanced insights into how this shift in perspective serves as a potent catalyst for enduring and substantial change.

Comprehending the wealth mindset is important for its cultivation. It goes beyond the mere pursuit of material wealth but encompasses a comprehensive outlook that covers various facets of life. Embracing opportunities involves being open to possibilities and acknowledging the abundance of paths for growth and success.

Skillfully navigating challenges involves fostering resilience and adaptability, perceiving obstacles not as barriers but as stepping stones toward personal growth. Immersing oneself in these foundational principles yields a profound comprehension of the wealth mindset, underscoring its transformative potential in catalyzing enduring and meaningful changes in one's life.

Rewiring Your Beliefs about Money

Exploring Limiting Beliefs

In your journey to foster a prosperous mindset, it's vital to reshape your perspectives on finances. This involves a thorough investigation to pinpoint and challenge restrictive beliefs that could hinder your economic progress. This helps to meticulously scrutinize the layers of our beliefs, recognizing their subtle yet influential barriers. It involves a deep dive, tracing back from childhood influences to societal conditioning, unveiling the roots of these limiting beliefs. This process provides you with the awareness and understanding necessary to deliberately reshape your connection with money, liberating yourself from constraints that may have obstructed wealth accumulation.

Hidden barriers linked to finances can quietly obstruct advancement, shaping your decisions and actions in financial affairs. By diligently recognizing and addressing these convictions, you develop a profound insight into the factors shaping your financial mindset. A thorough exploration of beliefs stemming from early experiences and societal norms offers a holistic approach to rewiring, enabling you to intentionally adjust your perspectives and attitudes toward money. This heightened awareness serves as a drive for positive change, paving the way for financial progress.

Strategies for Building Sustainable Wealth

Financial Education and Empowerment:

In the complex realm of finance, possessing knowledge emerges as a formidable asset. Emphasis on the critical role of financial education in the pursuit of enduring wealth. Going beyond traditional approaches, it goes into the core of comprehending investment principles and navigating the ever-evolving market trends. The objective of this segment is to empower individuals by imparting essential knowledge, equipping them to make informed and strategic financial decisions in line with their overarching wealth-building aspirations.

Setting precise financial objectives is an important step towards attaining long-lasting wealth. This entails dissecting overarching goals into specific, measurable, attainable, relevant, and time-bound (SMART) targets. Strategic planning ensures a well-defined trajectory, incorporating pragmatic steps aligned with the broader wealth-building strategy. This structured approach not only provides guidance but also enhances the ability to confront challenges, stay aligned with financial objectives, and navigate the complexities of establishing enduring wealth.

Nurturing a Wealth Mindset in Daily Life

Practicing Mindfulness and Gratitude

Building a mindset for wealth involves more than financial strategies; it incorporates habits of mindfulness and gratitude. These routines serve as effective tools to anchor your mindset in the present. Mindfulness is about being fully present and aware, enabling you to appreciate the depth of each moment. Gratitude, on the other hand, prompts you to acknowledge and be thankful for the abundance already existing in your life. Integrating these practices creates a mental environment that fosters positivity and a deeper connection with your wealth, going beyond its mere monetary value.

Mindfulness helps you focus on the present, preventing stress about the future or lingering concerns from the past. Gratitude shifts your perspective from scarcity to abundance, fostering contentment and positivity.

Creating a Supportive Environment:
Maintaining a wealthy mindset is closely linked to the environment you build around yourself. This includes both your physical surroundings and the people you interact with daily. Community, mentorship, and positive influences play key roles in shaping your financial journey. Being part of a supportive community provides encouragement, shared experiences, and diverse

perspectives. Mentorship offers guidance from those with valuable insights and experiences, creating a roadmap for overcoming financial challenges. Positive influences contribute to a mindset that embraces opportunities and sees setbacks as stepping stones toward growth. Recognizing the profound impact of your environment on your mindset is important for achieving lasting success in your financial pursuits.

The environment you place yourself in, significantly influences your mindset and, consequently, your financial success. A supportive community offers understanding and shared wisdom, while mentorship provides guidance based on real-world experiences. Surrounding yourself with positive influences encourages a mindset that perceives challenges as opportunities for learning and growth. Understanding and actively cultivating this supportive environment is transformative in sustaining a wealth mindset throughout your daily life.

Chapter 3

Introduction to a High-Converting Website

Welcome to an immersive journey into crafting a website with top-notch conversion rates—an essential ingredient in unlocking the "Path to Millionaire Status Through Affiliate Marketing." In this segment, we'll dive deep into the intricacies of building a website that not only attracts visitors but also effectively turns them into actively engaged, paying customers. By recognizing the undeniable power of a well-optimized site, we're ready to reveal strategies that will significantly boost your efforts in the world of affiliate marketing.

Having a website that converts well is more than just drawing in traffic; it serves as a game-changer, transforming casual visitors into valuable contributors to your affiliate marketing triumphs. Understanding this crucial role lays the groundwork for the strategies to come, emphasizing the direct impact that conversions can have on your financial objectives and long-term successes in the affiliate marketing realm. Together, we'll navigate the complexities of creating a website that not only resonates with visitors but also propels you toward the coveted millionaire status we all aspire to reach.

Building a user friendly website

Improving User Experience:

Elevating your website's effectiveness, especially in driving conversions, begins with prioritizing a user-friendly interface. This involves mastering the art of seamless navigation to ensure every visitor can effortlessly explore your site. Elements like intuitive menus and strategically positioned calls-to-action are pivotal in fostering a positive user experience, ultimately leading to higher conversion rates.

Ensuring mobile compatibility goes beyond a technical requirement; it's a strategic move to engage a wider audience. Explore different practical steps to make your website responsive, considering the diverse range of devices your audience uses. This not only enhances user experience but also positions your site for success.

Optimizing Content Strategies for Conversions

For individuals willing to go into affiliate marketing, you should know how important it is to create content that really grabs attention. Let's explore some fresh approaches to crafting content that goes beyond just giving information – content that really persuades. Like using the art of storytelling, strategically placing those affiliate links, and why it's so crucial to always deliver real value to your audience.

Now, let's talk visuals:

You know how powerful visuals can be in capturing attention and keeping people interested, right? Let's explore some advanced strategies for seamlessly weaving eye-catching visuals into your content – think captivating images, informative infographics, and engaging videos. These elements are more than just decorations; they're strategic tools to make your website visually appealing and boost those conversion rates.

And remember, visual appeal is key to keeping your audience engaged. Let's talk about how carefully chosen visuals can really elevate your content, making it easier to understand and more memorable for your audience. From choosing the perfect images to creating impactful infographics and videos, each element helps tell a story that resonates with your audience and drives those conversion rates.

Enhancing Conversion with Strategic Techniques

Let's explore the art of crafting compelling calls-to-action (CTAs) together. We'll uncover techniques that boost conversions by mastering the skill of creating persuasive CTAs. Discover the psychology behind these powerful elements and learn how to strategically incorporate them throughout your website. You'll see how well-crafted CTAs can smoothly guide you toward desired actions, significantly boosting your conversion rates.

Understanding the psychology behind CTAs means noticing subtle cues that prompt users to take specific actions. Dive into the nuances of crafting persuasive language, injecting urgency, and aligning CTAs with the user journey. Thoughtful placement ensures these prompts are visible and strategically positioned, increasing the likelihood of visitor engagement and conversion.

Analyzing and Iterating for Continuous Improvement

Understanding your website's analytics is like having a guiding light in the digital world. uncovering valuable insights into how users behave, the flow of traffic, and the rate at which visitors convert. Armed with this invaluable information, you can confidently make informed decisions to continuously improve your website, enhancing its overall performance.

Keep learning and adapting to new techniques in utilizing analytical tools to understand user behavior, spot traffic trends, and evaluate conversion rates. This understanding is a powerful asset, giving you the clarity needed to refine your website's strategic optimization, ensuring it stays in line with changing trends, audience preferences, and industry dynamics. Remember, constant improvement is key to long-term success in the ever-changing landscape of affiliate marketing.

Chapter 4.

Effective Content Marketing Strategies

When it comes to affiliate marketing, the primary influence rests within the uniqueness of your contents. The effectiveness of your affiliate pursuits is greatly shaped by the success of your content marketing strategy. After comprehending the traits of your target audience and understanding their needs, create content that not only highlights your products but also provides significant value and pragmatic solutions.

Creating Engaging and SEO-Optimized Content

To improve your experience in affiliate marketing and achieve superior outcomes, prioritize creating content that captivates your audience while also being optimized for search engines (SEO). Invest time in thorough keyword research to uncover pertinent terms within your niche. Skillfully incorporate these keywords into your content to ensure a smooth reading experience. Craft attention-grabbing headlines and meta descriptions to boost click-through rates. By seamlessly integrating engaging content with SEO principles, you expand the visibility of your affiliate links, drawing in a broader audience..

Building Authority through Educational Content

Another strategy to broaden your reach and boost your earnings in affiliate marketing involves establishing yourself as an expert in your particular niche. Produce informative content that tackles common questions or issues within your audience, whether through tutorials, comprehensive guides, or detailed product reviews. By consistently providing valuable information, you cultivate trust and credibility, fostering a more receptive attitude towards your affiliate suggestions. Educational content not only informs but also persuades, leading to increased conversion rates for your affiliate links.

Leveraging Multiple Content Channels for Maximum Impact

Broaden the distribution of your content across various channels to engage a larger audience. Utilize social media platforms, email marketing, and guest posting to enhance the visibility of your content. Tailor your strategy for each platform, considering the unique preferences of your audience. Experiment with different content formats, such as videos, infographics, and podcasts, to cater to diverse preferences. Through strategic use of multiple channels, not only will you expand your reach, but you'll also strengthen your overall content marketing strategy, enhancing the effectiveness of your affiliate marketing efforts.

Remember, the essence of a successful content marketing strategy in affiliate marketing lies in providing value, building trust, and adapting to the ever-changing landscape. Continuously assess the performance of your content, stay abreast of industry trends, and refine your approach to ensure lasting success in your affiliate marketing endeavors.

Selecting appropriate affiliate programs is a pivotal step in launching a prosperous affiliate marketing enterprise. Begin by understanding the intricacies of various affiliate programs. Seek out programs that match your niche and appeal to your intended audience. Conduct a thorough evaluation of the reputation and dependability of affiliate programs, verifying a history of equitable commission payments and transparent operations.

Researching and Evaluating Affiliate Programs

Before committing to any affiliate program, it's essential to conduct extensive research. Take a close look at the products or services available, commission rates, and cookie durations. Assess the reputation of the merchants and the terms of their affiliate programs. Opt for programs that offer robust tracking and reporting tools, making it easy to monitor your performance effectively. Evaluating the potential earnings and long-term viability of the program is crucial for a sustainable and lucrative affiliate marketing venture.

Building Relationships with Merchants

Achieving success in affiliate marketing goes beyond mere transactions; it requires building strong relationships with merchants. It's crucial for long-term success. Start conversations with merchants to understand their objectives, marketing strategies, and target audience. Demonstrate your dedication to effectively promoting their products. Establishing transparent communication channels fosters a collaborative environment, allowing you to access support, exclusive promotions, and valuable insights that can enhance your affiliate marketing efforts.

Diversification and Adapting Strategies

To minimize risks and maximize revenue opportunities, refrain from solely concentrating on one affiliate program. Diversify your income sources by tapping into multiple revenue streams. Remain vigilant of industry trends and be prepared to adjust your strategies as needed. Monitor shifts in commission rates, product availability, and market conditions. By maintaining flexibility and adaptability, you set yourself up for success in the ever-changing realm of affiliate marketing. Keep in mind that the essence lies not only in affiliating with programs but also in fostering meaningful relationships that foster mutual growth.

Chapter 5

Mastering SEO for Affiliate Success

Start with understanding the basics of Search Engine Optimization (SEO) it is essential for attaining success in affiliate marketing. Start by understanding the role of SEO in driving organic traffic to your affiliate links. Begin by decoding the importance of keywords, meta tags, and high-quality content in optimizing your website for search engines. A strong understanding of SEO principles lays the groundwork for a successful affiliate marketing strategy.

Keyword Research and Implementation

A vital component of effective SEO involves mastering the art of identifying relevant keywords in your niche, utilizing tools like Google Keyword Planner and SEMrush. Utilize different methods of seamlessly integrating these keywords into your content, ensuring a smooth and reader-friendly experience. By mastering the techniques of keyword research and implementation, you enhance the visibility of your affiliate content, attracting users actively seeking the products or services you promote.

Off-Page SEO and Link Building Strategies

Broaden your expertise in SEO to encompass off-page tactics and strategies for building links. Recognize the importance of backlinks in demonstrating authority to search engines. Acquire knowledge about ethical and efficient approaches to obtaining backlinks, including guest posting, engaging with influencers, and actively participating in relevant communities. A strong off-page SEO strategy complements your on-page efforts, contributing to improved search engine rankings and bolstering overall credibility.

Monitoring, Analytics, and Continuous Improvement

Remember, SEO is a constantly evolving field, and staying updated on algorithm changes and industry trends ensures the ongoing effectiveness of your affiliate marketing endeavors. Mastering SEO for affiliate success is an ongoing endeavor that requires a deep comprehension of SEO principles, adept keyword research, optimized content creation, and strategic off-page techniques. By consistently refining and adapting your methods, you position yourself for long-term success in the competitive world of affiliate marketing.

Social Media Tactics for Millionaire Affiliate Marketers

Becoming a successful millionaire affiliate marketer involves maximizing the vast opportunities presented by social media platforms. Recognize the significance of social media in broadening your audience, establishing a brand presence, and driving traffic to your affiliate links. This segment aims to acquaint you with the influence of social media and lay the groundwork for delving into the precise strategies adopted by accomplished affiliate marketers.

Choosing the Right Social Media Platforms

There exist Significant distinctions among various social media platforms. It's crucial to explore strategies for choosing platforms that align with your niche and target demographic to guarantee success. Evaluate the distinctive characteristics and user demographics of prominent platforms like Instagram, Facebook, Twitter, and LinkedIn. Grasping the intricacies of each platform and its algorithm enables you to customize your strategy and optimize your presence on the platforms that best align with your affiliate marketing objectives.

Building an Engaging Social Media Presence

Building a solid presence on social media goes beyond just sharing affiliate links. Explore a variety of strategies employed by successful affiliate marketers to craft engaging content. Additionally, closely examine the methods of skilled affiliate marketers, understanding their tactics and adjusting your own approach to achieve desired results. Explore techniques such as storytelling, visual appeal, and interactive elements to captivate your audience. Master the art of maintaining a balance between promotional content and valuable, shareable information to cultivate a loyal following.

Strategic Content Planning and Scheduling

Effectively strategize and organize your social media content to achieve optimal impact. Develop a content calendar, incorporate thematic planning, and emphasize the significance of consistency, acknowledging it as a crucial factor for positive outcomes. Consistency is key if you aspire to achieve results akin to those of millionaire affiliates. Explore automation tools that simplify content creation and scheduling, enabling you to uphold an active and engaging presence without feeling overwhelmed. A well-planned content strategy guarantees that your affiliate marketing messages resonate with your audience, ensuring continuous visibility and alignment with your overall brand identity.

Utilizing Paid Advertising on Social Media

Successful affiliate marketers often leverage paid promotions to expand their reach and attract targeted visitors. Unlike organic reach constrained by algorithms, paid advertising ensures broad visibility without relying on follower engagement. It opens up endless possibilities for your content to consistently reach new audiences. Learn effective strategies for creating social media ad campaigns by understanding algorithm mechanics, refining precise targeting for your desired audience, and mastering budget allocation and A/B testing for optimal performance. Explore sponsored posts, influencer partnerships, and other paid methods to enhance your affiliate marketing successes. For beginners, starting with organic traffic is recommended, allowing you to generate income before venturing into paid ads to significantly increase earnings.

Analytics, Optimization, and Scaling Strategies

Delve into social media strategies emphasizing analytics, optimization, and scalability. Cultivate the skill to dissect social media metrics, pinpointing successful tactics and areas needing improvement. Examine optimization techniques aligned with audience behavior and engagement metrics.

As you refine your approach, grasp how to strategically expand your social media efforts, ensuring steady growth and increased affiliate revenue. For flourishing affiliate marketers, mastery of social media tactics entails a strategic blend of platform selection, content creation, paid advertising, and ongoing optimization. By integrating these elements into your affiliate marketing strategy, you unlock the full potential of social media, propelling yourself toward millionaire status.

Optimizing Paid Advertising for Maximum ROI

Understanding the effectiveness of paid advertising is crucial for success in affiliate marketing and reaching millionaire status. Assessing the return on investment (ROI) before using paid advertising is important because it helps improve visibility, attract targeted audiences, and increase revenue for affiliate marketers.

Understanding Paid Advertising Platforms

Maximize the effectiveness of paid advertising by first understanding the diverse advertising platforms available. Explore commonly used options like Google

Ads, Facebook Ads, and native advertising platforms, each providing unique features, targeting options, and ad formats. Develop a clear understanding of the strengths and limitations of each platform, so you can make informed decisions that align with your affiliate marketing goals.

Crafting Compelling Ad Copy and Creatives

Refine your skills in creating impactful ad text and captivating visuals. Learn how to attract attention with attention-grabbing headlines, concise messages, and visually appealing graphics. Understand the significance of aligning your ad content with the interests and needs of your target audience. Recognizing what your audience wants is important for offering solutions they may not even realize they need. Use A/B testing regularly to fine-tune your ad elements, ensuring that your paid campaigns continuously evolve for optimal effectiveness.

Strategic Audience Targeting for Precise Reach

Efficiently reaching the intended audience is important for anyone trying to maximize the impact of paid advertising efforts. Pinpointing the ideal audience precisely amplifies the efficacy and affordability of your paid advertising endeavors.

Budgeting and Bid Optimization Techniques

Budget management and bid optimization is essential for attaining a substantial return on investment in paid advertising. Without a well-defined budget, advertising costs can spiral out of control.

Establish practical budgets aligned with your objectives and monitor campaign effectiveness against these financial outlines. Explore different bidding approaches like manual, automated, and bid adjustments. Acquire proficiency in strategically distributing your budget across multiple campaigns and channels to enhance ROI.

Analytics, Conversion Tracking, and Continuous Improvement

To maximize ROI in affiliate marketing through paid advertising, it's important to adopt a strategic approach. This involves choosing platforms, crafting ads, pinpointing target audiences, budgeting effectively, and continuously analyzing performance. By integrating these components into your paid advertising strategy, you set yourself up for success in the competitive landscape of affiliate marketing.

Chapter 6

Taking an affiliate business to millionaire heights necessitates a systematic and strategic approach. Commence by comprehending the notion of scaling and its impacts in the domain of affiliate marketing. This section highlights the importance of scalability, accentuating the potential for increased revenue, expanded market outreach, and overall business growth.

Establishing a Solid Foundation for Scaling

Before going into strategies for expansion, ensure that your affiliate business has a strong foundation. Consider the significance of a well-optimized website, resilient affiliate partnerships, and a diverse range of products. Verify the functionality of your tracking and analytics systems to accurately measure performance. Building a robust foundation lays the groundwork for successful growth without compromising the integrity of your business.

Automating and Outsourcing Routine Tasks

Efficiently grow your affiliate business by automating routine tasks and delegating non-essential activities to external parties. Consider the use of tools designed to automate tasks such as email marketing, social media scheduling, and analytics reporting. Evaluate outsourcing options for tasks that don't align with your core strengths, enabling you to concentrate on the strategic facets of your business. This segment outlines the advantages and recommended approaches for integrating automation and outsourcing into the domain of affiliate marketing.

Analyzing Data, Iterating, and Sustaining Growth

The final step in growing your affiliate business is to keep analyzing data, improving strategies, and growing consistently. Learn to understand performance numbers, see patterns, and make smart decisions based on data. Keep tweaking your methods, trying new things, and adapting to changes in affiliate marketing. By always aiming to get better, your affiliate business can become really successful and keep growing over time.

Networking in Affiliate Marketing

Networking in affiliate marketing means more than just going to events or swapping business cards. It's about building real relationships. Connect with experienced marketers through webinars and online forums to learn from their experiences. Join social media groups and industry conferences to stay involved. Talk to people, share ideas, ask questions, and show that you're a valuable part of the community. Good networking can lead to partnerships, mentors, and valuable knowledge.

Identifying and Connecting with Potential Partner

Strategic alliances frequently act as the catalyst for rapid growth in affiliate marketing. Delve into diverse methods and procedures to pinpoint and establish connections with potential partners. Investigate approaches for researching and assessing potential collaborators, ensuring alignment with your niche, audience, and business values. Refine your skill in crafting personalized and persuasive partnership proposals, emphasizing the mutual benefits of collaboration. Recognizing and establishing connections with the appropriate partners sets the foundation for synergistic relationships, propelling you on the path to achieving millionaire status.

Nurturing and Sustaining Strategic Partnership

Teamwork is key for fast growth in affiliate marketing. Learn how to find and connect with potential partners. Make sure they fit your niche, audience, and values. Get good at making partnership proposals that show how working together benefits everyone. Finding the right partners sets you up for success.

Measuring Partnership Success and Evolving Strategies

Consider figuring out how to see if your partnerships are working and getting better at connecting with others.

Decide what important things you want to keep track of, like more people coming to your site, more of them buying stuff, and how much money you're making. Learn how to change your plans based on how things are going and what's happening in the market. By always checking and getting better at how you connect and partner up, you make sure your affiliate marketing journey doesn't just hit the big time, but keeps doing well even when things get tough.

Chapter 7

Like any business, aiming to become a millionaire through affiliate marketing comes with its own set of challenges. But challenges also bring opportunities. Let's explore the common obstacles faced by affiliate marketers and understand how resilience and motivation are key to overcoming them.

Identifying Common Challenges in Affiliate Marketing

Start by looking at the problems affiliate marketers face, like lots of competition, changes in how websites rank, and shifts in what people like. Remember, what people want can change over time. Understand how these things affect your business and know that overcoming challenges is part of reaching millionaire status. Also, keep up with what's happening in the market and what people like, so you can stay ahead and keep making money consistently.

Strategies for Overcoming Challenges

Learn practical ways to overcome challenges in affiliate marketing. Stay updated on industry changes, find new sources of traffic, and adjust strategies to fit algorithm updates. Keep learning and be flexible to succeed in the changing landscape. These methods help affiliate marketers turn problems into opportunities for growth.

Resilience and Persistence

For affiliate marketers aiming to become millionaires, it's essential to be persistent and determined. Let's talk about the attitude needed to face challenges with resilience. Look at real stories of successful marketers who kept going despite setbacks, especially with the help of a strong network. This shows how important it is to stay strong during tough times.

Staying Motivated on the Millionaire Journey

To overcome challenges, it's important to stay motivated. Understand what keeps you going and find ways to maintain your enthusiasm. Remember why you started affiliate marketing, set achievable goals, celebrate small wins, and visualize your success. By staying motivated, you can keep pushing forward toward your financial goals.

Building a Support Systems

Affiliate marketers often deal with personal challenges that can affect their mental well-being. It's important to have support, like mentors, networking groups, or online communities. Being around like-minded people gives advice, motivation, and a sense of belonging, making it easier to overcome hurdles on the journey to becoming a millionaire.

Evolving and Thriving Despite Challenges

Succeeding despite challenges is important. When faced with obstacles, successful affiliate marketers adapt their strategies and keep moving forward. By staying motivated, building a supportive network, and tackling challenges head-on, you can confidently pursue your goal of becoming a millionaire.

CONCLUSION:

Navigating the Road to Affiliate Millionaire Success

In our exploration of "Secrets to making millions with affiliate marketing," we've unveiled the essential principles that outline the journey from beginner to affiliate marketing millionaire. From grasping the basics in the "Introduction to Affiliate Marketing" to overcoming obstacles and staying motivated during tough times, each section adds to a complete guide for those aiming for millionaire status through affiliate marketing.

'A Millionaire's blueprints' is more than just a series of chapters; it serves as a roadmap filled with practical insights and strategies. By emphasizing the importance of adopting a wealth mindset, providing advice on creating a high-performing website, and simplifying the complexities of content marketing and SEO, this book gives you the tools to take your affiliate businesses to new heights.

More Resources

Affiliate Marketing Programs and Platforms

As you start or continue your journey toward reaching millionaire status in affiliate marketing, explore these reputable affiliate marketing programs and platforms to gain extra support and opportunities.:

1. Amazon's Affiliate Program: A leader in the realm of affiliate marketing, Amazon's program boasts an extensive product selection and robust tracking capabilities.

2. ClickBank: Recognized for its focus on digital goods, ClickBank offers a broad marketplace featuring lucrative commission structures.

3. Commission Junction (CJ): A global platform for affiliate marketing, CJ serves as a conduit between marketers and leading brands across multiple sectors.

4. Rakuten Advertising: Providing a vast array of products and services, Rakuten presents affiliates with diverse earning possibilities.

5. ShareASale: Facilitating connections between affiliates and merchants, ShareASale offers an intuitive platform for collaboration.

6. Awin: Linking affiliates with advertisers worldwide, Awin operates as a comprehensive affiliate marketing network.

7. MaxBounty: Specializing in CPA marketing, MaxBounty stands out for its varied and high-performing offers.

8. Shopify Affiliate Program: Tailored for e-commerce enthusiasts, the Shopify Affiliate Program offers commissions for promoting their solutions.

9. JVZoo: Focused on digital products, JVZoo enables affiliates to promote and earn from a range of online courses, software, and digital assets.

10. TradeDoubler: With a global presence, TradeDoubler provides affiliates with opportunities to promote diverse products and services.

11. Admitad: Operating in multiple countries, Admitad connects affiliates with a wide array of advertisers, alongside advanced tracking and reporting tools.

12. VigLink: Converting regular product links into affiliate links, VigLink offers a seamless monetization option for bloggers and content creators.

13. FlexOffers: Spanning various industries, FlexOffers links affiliates with a broad spectrum of advertisers, fostering numerous earning avenues.

Achieving millionaire status through affiliate marketing demands a combination of skill, perseverance, and thoughtful implementation. This guide serves as a comprehensive handbook to navigate the challenging yet rewarding journey. As you delve into the world of affiliate marketing, remember that triumph stems from continuous education, flexibility, and the determination to surmount challenges. May your endeavors in affiliate marketing not only bring financial abundance but also realize your entrepreneurial dreams.

www.ingramcontent.com/pod-product-compliance
Lightning Source LLC
Chambersburg PA
CBHW071057290526
45795CB00004B/1532